HUMMINGBIRDS CAN FLY BACKWARDS

I Bet You Didn't Know That...

HUMMINGBIRDS CAN FLY BACKWARDS

and Other Facts and Curiosities

by Carol Iverson • pictures by Jack Lindstrom

 Lerner Publications Company • Minneapolis

With thanks to Gary DeGrote and his sixth graders,
Addi Engen, Isabel Marvin, Joan Ennis, Torild
Homstad, and my husband, Art

Library of Congress Cataloging-in-Publication Data

Iverson, Carol.
 Hummingbirds can fly backwards and other facts and curiosities /
Carol Iverson ; pictures by Jack Lindstrom.
  p. cm. – (I bet you didn't know that)
 Summary: A collection of miscellaneous facts about nature,
animals, plants, and the human body.
  ISBN 0-8225-2276-4 (lib. bdg.)
  1. Animals – Miscellanea – Juvenile literature 2. Plants –
Miscellanea – Juvenile literature. 3. Human biology – Miscellanea –
Juvenile literature. [1. Animals – Miscellanea. 2. Plants –
Miscellanea. 3. Body, Human – Miscellanea. 4. Curiosities and
wonders.] I. Lindstrom, Jack, ill. II. Title. III. Series: Iverson, Carol.
I bet you didn't know that.
QL49.I94   1990
574 – dc20   89-27182
                                                       CIP
                                                        AC

Manufactured in the United States of America

1 2 3 4 5 6 7 8 9 10 99 98 97 96 95 94 93 92 91 90

I Bet You Didn't Know That...

A banana is about 75 percent water.

I Bet You Didn't Know That...

Eighty percent of the human brain is water.

Children grow faster in the springtime than they do during the rest of the year.

The average person loses from 50 to 100 strands of hair each day.

Your hair grows faster during the summer than it does in the winter.

You use only about 17 muscles to smile, but you need more than 40 to frown.

There are 206 bones in the human body – 54 of these are in the hands.

A baby has over 60 bones more than an adult.

I Bet You Didn't Know That...

The average person spends over 20 years of his or her life sleeping.

Humans are the only animals that sleep on their backs.

Kangaroos can cover 40 feet
(12 meters) with one jump
and can jump 10 feet (3 m)
into the air.

The kangaroo was named when
English explorer Captain James
Cook asked native Australians
the name of the animal. They
answered, "kangaroo," which
meant that they didn't under-
stand Cook's question.

I Bet You Didn't Know That...

Just like fingerprints, no two lip-prints are exactly alike.

No two leopard skins are identical in their markings.

Cattle can be identified by their nose-prints.

The hurricane plant is protected from destruction in high winds because it has holes in its leaves that let the wind come through.

One Native American legend says that water lilies are fallen stars.

The leaves of a giant South American water lily are so strong that they will hold a person.

I Bet You Didn't Know That...

Ermine is the white, winter fur of the weasel.

The porcupine has over 20,000 quills. It does not shoot them at its attackers. The quills stick to the victim by a barbed end and easily come off the porcupine's body.

To keep from drifting away in the water while it sleeps, the sea otter wraps itself in seaweed that is attached to rocks or the sea floor.

The sloth, a mammal of the South American rain forests, can turn its head around 270 degrees.

A kitten is born blind and deaf.

The lowest branch of a redwood tree can be 150 feet (45 m) off the ground.

Trees never stop growing.

The cones on a spruce tree grow downwards, and the cones on a fir tree grow upwards.

I Bet You Didn't Know That...

The average child usually doubles his or her birth height by age 5 or 6. By age 12 or 13, a child's birth height has tripled.

The chance of a pregnant woman giving birth to twins is 1 in 90.

70,000 MI.

A sneeze can come out of your mouth at almost 100 miles per hour (160 kilometers per hour).

You are taller in the morning than you are at night – sometimes by as much as an inch (2.5 centimeters).

A person begins to shrink in height after about age 30.

Between childhood and old age, you will walk about 70,000 miles (112,000 km).

I Bet You Didn't Know That...

An elephant eats about 600 pounds (270 kg) of food and drinks 30 to 50 gallons (114 to 190 liters) of water a day.

A newborn elephant weighs about 200 pounds (90 kilograms) and stands three feet (90 cm) tall.

The elephant is the only animal with four knees.

The giraffe is the tallest animal in the world. It can grow to be 19 feet (570 cm) tall.

A giraffe has the same number of vertebrae in its neck as a person has: seven.

I Bet You Didn't Know That...

An ear of corn always has an even number
of rows.

The strawberry is a member of the rose family.

The tangerine is also known as the kid glove orange.

Lemons contain more sugar than strawberries do.

Grapefruit probably got its name because the fruits grow in bunches like grapes.

In 1893, the Supreme Court declared that the tomato is a vegetable, not a fruit.

I Bet You Didn't Know That...

Sloths are the slowest mammals. They travel at a top speed of 0.1 miles an hour (.16 km/h).

Gorillas are peace-loving and would rather retreat than fight.

The warmer the
climate, the longer a
jack rabbit's ears are.

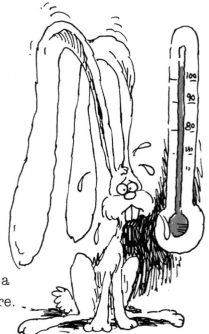

The giant panda was not known by scientists
until 1869.

A newborn panda weighs only five ounces
(140 grams).

I Bet You Didn't Know That...

The average yield of a coffee tree is one pound (.45 kg) of coffee beans per year.

The camel's hump is used to store fat, not water.

The camel can close its nostrils during a sandstorm. It also has three eyelids on each eye: two to keep out the sand and one to wipe off the dust.

A hippopotamus can weigh up to four tons and can run as fast as a person.

A good dairy cow gives about 5,000 quarts (4,750 l) of milk a year.

I Bet You Didn't Know That...

You dream at least three dreams a night and as many as nine.

Most people move approximately once every 10 minutes when they sleep.

About half of the people say that they dream in color.

The tip of your tongue is sensitive to sweets, the back is sensitive to bitter tastes, and the sides are sensitive to salty and sour tastes.

The human body has over 600 muscles and 40 miles (64 km) of nerves.

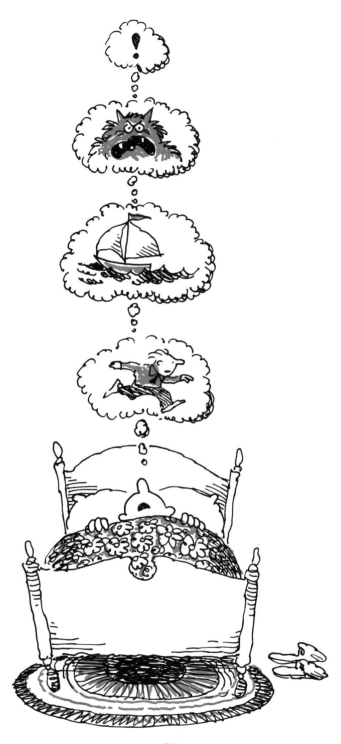

I Bet You Didn't Know That...

Once there were about 60 million buffalo in North America.

King Henry VIII once ordered that all horses less than five feet (150 cm) tall be destroyed.

A full-grown Chinese water deer stands only 21 inches (52.5 cm) at the shoulder.

The royal antelope of Africa is only 10 inches (25 cm) high at the shoulder.

I Bet You Didn't Know That...

The iris plant was named for the goddess of the rainbow, Iris.

The goldenrod was once suggested as the national flower of the United States.

At one time the tulip grew only in Turkey. Tulip is the Turkish word for turban.

The largest flower in the world is the giant rafflesia. It grows up to 3 feet (90 cm) across and can weigh 15 pounds (6.75 kg).

I Bet You Didn't Know That...

The fastest land animal in the world is the cheetah. It can run a mile (1.6 km) in less than a minute.

The giant tortoise of the Galapagos Islands can weigh up to 500 pounds (225 kg).

The tortoise is the longest-lived animal. It can live to be 100 years old.

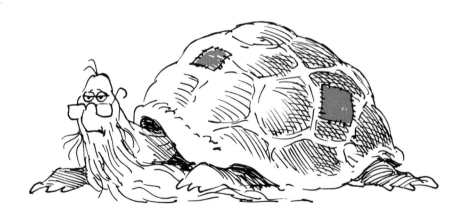

Unlike most members of the cat family, tigers
are good swimmers.

Hummingbirds can fly backwards. While most
birds can only flap their wings up and down,
the hummingbird can rotate its wings in a
figure-eight pattern. This allows the bird to
fly backwards and hover like a helicopter.

About the Author

Carol Iverson has been collecting interesting facts and trivia for the **I Bet You Didn't Know That** books for many years. Formerly a dental assistant, Iverson now spends much of her time writing for children. She lives in Northfield, Minnesota, with her husband, Art.

About the Artist

Artist **Jack Lindstrom** is a native of Minneapolis and a partner in a Minneapolis art studio. Lindstrom graduated from the Minneapolis College of Art and Design and currently illustrates a syndicated comic strip for United Features.

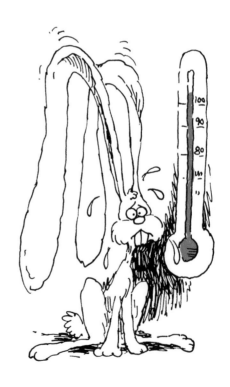